Raccoon Butterflyfish

Cardinalfish

Convict Tang

Crocodile Needlefish

Flying Gurnard

Forktail Snapper

Frogfish

Goatfish

Hawaiian Lionfish

Leatherback

Milkfish

Moorish Idol

Reef Triggerfish

Rudderfish

Sailfin Tang

Scorpionfish

KNOW YOUR FISHES IN HAWAI'I

Surgeonfish at WORK

A Fun Fish Identification Book for Kids

WILFRED TOKI

Photographs by **JOHN P. HOOVER & KEOKI STENDER**

BEACHHOUSE
Publishing, LLC

Dedicated to Oliver Toki, Dominique Wijaya and Jacqueline Wijaya

Library of Congress Catalog Card
Number: 2004103221

ISBN -10: 0-9729905-9-3
ISBN-13: 978-0-9729905-9-2
First Printing, June 2005
Second Printing, April 2008

BeachHouse Publishing, LLC
PO Box 2926
`Ewa Beach, Hawai`i 96706
email: info@beachhousepublishing.com
www.beachhousepublishing.com

Printed in Korea

INTRODUCTION

Hawai'i's waters are home to hundreds of beautiful, colorful, strange, and wonderful fishes—from the **BIG EYE EMPEROR** whose teeth look like human molars to the **FLYING GURNARD** that doesn't actually fly. How can anyone remember all their names?

Now you can. Here are over forty of Hawai'i's most unique and interesting fishes drawn in a fun way to help you remember their names. Picture the **SURGEONFISH** with a surgeon's mask and scalpel; picture the **TRUMPETFISH** playing (what else?) a trumpet and you'll be able to remember its name the next time you're out snorkeling or fishing.

You'll also learn what they look like, what they eat, how they act, and which ones are beautiful, weird, gross, or plain creepy.

Many of these fish played an important role in ancient Hawai'i. Did you know that the **LEATHERBACK'S** skin was dried, stretched, and used to make the tops of drums? What do you know about **WHITESADDLE GOATFISH**? They were a prized fish in old Hawai'i and sometimes used in offerings if a pig couldn't be found.

There's so much to learn about all the fish out there! Next time you go snorkeling, you can impress your friends and family. Instead of saying, "Hey look, a striped fish!" you can say, "Hey look, it's a manini!"

Most of all, you'll find out why Hawai'i's unofficial state fish, the Reef Triggerfish or **HUMUHUMUNUKUNUKUĀPUA'A**, is so cool. It's not just because it has a super long name.

BEARDED CUSK EEL
PUHI PALAHOANA

John P. Hoover

Bearded Cusk Eels are very **SHY** and only come out at night when it's time to eat. They are dark reddish-brown with a long, flat body. Even though their "beards" look like cat whiskers, they are not. They are called **BARBELS** and they act as sensors helping them sense other animals and things around them, which is useful in the dark.

Did YOU KNoW?

Cusk Eels are not "true" eels. They belong to a different scientific order—Ophidiiformes.

John P. Hoover

Bigeye Emperors have **BIG** eyes compared to most other fishes. The adult fish are silver. Some of them have stripes. They eat at night. During the day, they stay around reefs. They move their fins and float in place, by the reef, without moving with the water's current. Younger fish like to swim closer to the bottom of the ocean. But the most interesting fact about these fish are their teeth. Mū have teeth that look like **HUMAN TEETH**— like molars, which are the big teeth in the back of our mouths!

CReEPY FACT! In ancient Hawai'i, the man sent to find victims to bury alive along with the body of a dead chief was called a mū.

BIGEYE 'ĀWEOWEO

John P. Hoover

Bigeye fish are bright red with **BIG** eyes (of course). They can change color if they are scared. They have oval-shaped bodies with upturned mouths, like a frown. You can find them in shallow reefs, and they eat at night. The Hawaiian name 'Āweoweo means **"GLOWING RED."** In ancient Hawai'i, if a large school of them was seen close to shore, it was a bad omen, or sign. It meant the future death of a chief.

WoW!
· · · · · ·
When King Kalākaua died, large schools of 'āweoweo could be seen gathered in Pearl Harbor making the water appear red!

6

BIRD WRASSE
HĪNĀLEA 'I'IWI

Bird Wrasses have long, curved snouts, just like the long, curved bill of the **'I'IWI**— the Hawaiian honeycreeper, which is a bird unique to Hawai'i. The shape of their snout helps them find food. They can use it to poke into small cracks in reefs to catch and eat small sea creatures. Their side fins move very fast, like the beating of a **BIRD'S WINGS**. The males are blue-green. Their Hawaiian name means "brain biting."

REaLLY? A long time ago, these fish were used to treat brain diseases in people!

7

RACCOON BUTTERFLYFISH
KĪKĀKAPU

John P. Hoover

Raccoon Butterflyfish look like they are wearing a mask—like a raccoon! They are orange-yellow with brown stripes. Young fish are brighter yellow than adult fish and have a **BLACK SPOT** by their tails which tricks other fish into thinking that's their **EYE**. They eat early in the morning in schools and spend the rest of the day relaxing. They can be found at Hanauma Bay on Oʻahu.

YuMMy Raccoon Butterflyfish like to eat algae. But, if you happen to have them in an aquarium, they really like chopped, frozen spinach!

CARDINALFISH
'UPĀPALU

John P. Hoover.

There are many different types of **Cardinalfish**. The one pictured above is called an **IRIDESCENT CARDINALFISH**. They are light brown, but at night, they are a shiny blue-green color. They have a dark stripe that runs through their eye right down to their tail. Some of the first Cardinalfish found were red—which is where they get their name. These fish can be found in Hawai`i's **SHALLOW WATERS**. They are most active at night when they hunt for food. During the day, they rest under reef ledges or in other dark places.

WeiRD FACT! The male Cardinalfish holds the female's eggs in his mouth up until they hatch. Sometimes his mouth can't close all the way because it's so full of eggs!

9

CONVICT
TANG
MANINI

John P. Hoover

Convict Tangs are light green with black stripes—like a convict's uniform. They are very **COMMON** in Hawai`i. The younger fish can be found in tidepools. There are a lot of them in Hanauma Bay on O`ahu. They eat algae and swim around reefs in big schools so they can overwhelm or crowd other fish trying to get food. In ancient Hawai`i the manini were a favorite dish. But later, the name manini was used to describe someone who was acting **STINGY**.

Did YOU KNoW? It's illegal for fishermen to catch baby manini. If they were caught, there would be no more manini!

CROCODILE NEEDLEFISH 'AHA

Needlefish are long and skinny with pointy snouts. **Crocodile Needlefish** are large with forked tails. They swim near the surface of the ocean. They are very strong swimmers. Some of them can **LEAP** out of the water like their cousins the flying fish, or mālolo. Fishermen have to be careful at night. Needlefish are attracted to light. If they get too excited, they might jump into a small boat and accidentally **STAB SOMEONE** with their needle-like beak! Ouch!

WoW! Crocodile Needlefish can grow more than three feet in length! That's one L O N G fish!

DEVILFISH
HĀHĀLUA

Keoki Stender

Devilfish is another name for manta rays. They are dark on the top and white underneath. Their bodies are flat with fins that look and act like underwater **WINGS**. They have long tails and two horns or flaps on the sides of their head that they use to eat with. The flaps scoop up microscopic plankton and guide the food into their mouths.

Did YOU KNoW? Some manta rays can be seen off the Kona coast of the Big Island.

FANTAIL FILEFISH
ʻŌʻILI ʻUWĪʻUWĪ

John P. Hoover

Fantail Filefish have rough skin and colorful fan-shaped tails—which is where they get their name. Just like Triggerfish, they can swim **BACKWARDS** or forwards. The Hawaiian name ʻōʻili which means "sprout" or "come up" describes the fish's dorsal spine which is often sticking up. The Fantail Filefish is a popular fish for home aquariums. But, watch them carefully. They will eat almost anything!

COoL! When a Fantail Filefish is taken out of the water, it makes a small noise, like a little squeal, which is what its name means in Hawaiian—to squeal. Another interesting fact is that in old Hawaiʻi, the dried bodies of these fish were sometimes used for fuel!

13

FLATFISH
PĀKIʻI

The most common **Flatfish** in Hawaiʻi are Peacock Flounders. They are light brown with spots. They have very **FLAT BODIES** which makes it easy for them to lie flat on the ocean floor. Because of their coloring, they blend in easily and are able to hide in the sand. The most interesting fact about them is their eyes. When young, their **EYES** are on either side of their heads, like normal fishes. And they swim straight, like normal fishes. But then they begin to lean to one side. Over time, one eye begins to move to the other side until both eyes are on the same side of their heads. When that happens, they can lie on the bottom of the ocean in the sand with both eyes looking up. Weird!

Did YOU KNoW? The Flatfish's Hawaiian name Pākiʻi means "fallen flat" or "spread out."

14

FLYING FISH
MĀLOLO

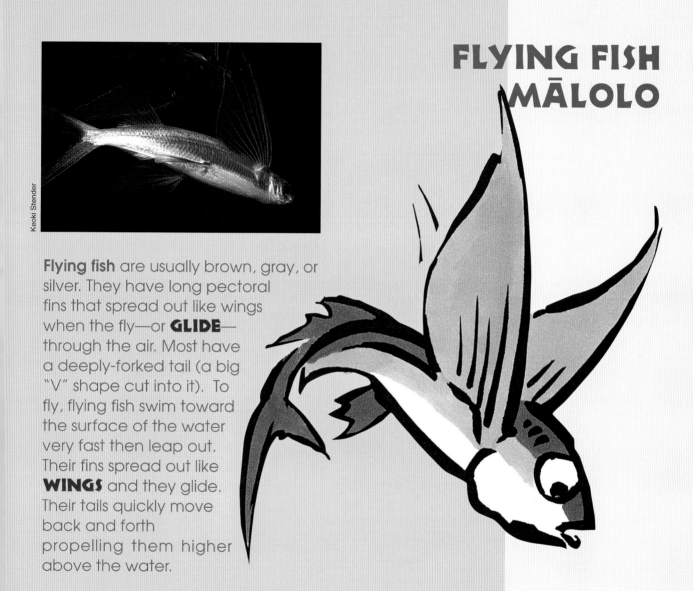

Flying fish are usually brown, gray, or silver. They have long pectoral fins that spread out like wings when the fly—or **GLIDE**—through the air. Most have a deeply-forked tail (a big "V" shape cut into it). To fly, flying fish swim toward the surface of the water very fast then leap out. Their fins spread out like **WINGS** and they glide. Their tails quickly move back and forth propelling them higher above the water.

REaLLY? The Hawaiian word mālolo also describes someone who is wishy-washy or "jumps" from relationship to relationship.

15

FLYING GURNARD
LOLOA'U

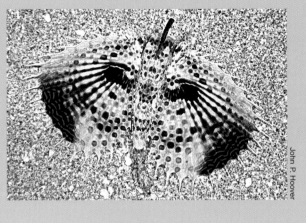

John P Hoover

Flying Gurnards are speckled to blend in with sand at the bottom of the sea. When scared, their large pectoral fins spread out like wings which helps them **BLEND IN** with the sand as they crawl along the ocean floor. Even though their name is Flying Gurnard, they **CANNOT FLY**. They hide in sandy channels along reefs and crawl using their fingerlike spines and fins.

WHeRE ARE THeY?

Hanauma Bay on O'ahu is a good place to try and see Flying Gurnards.

16

FORKTAIL SNAPPER WAHANUI

Forktail Snappers are usually a dark, silvery gray color. They have large mouths that are upturned, like frowns, and their tails are forked. They swim near the bottoms of reefs and can grow up to twelve inches long. They usually swim alone. Their Hawaiian name, Wahanui, means "**BIG MOUTH**."

WoW! There are about 100 species of snappers in the world. Hawai'i is home to thirteen of them.

17

FROGFISH

John P. Hoover

The Commerson's **Frogfish** are bigger than other Frogfish. They are splotchy colored to blend into rocks and coral reefs. But when they are young (like the one pictured above), they can be bright yellow, orange, or red. They can sit in one spot for a long time and because of their color, can blend in and hide in the reef or look just like a bright **SEA SPONGE**. Their fins act like hands or feet, holding onto coral. They like to stay in deep, deep waters, but some of the smaller types of Frogfish do well in aquariums. Watch closely. If they are kept in captivity, they might change color.

WeLL, LA, DEE, Da!

The Commerson Frogfish is named after a French biologist Philibert Commerson.

GOATFISH MOANO

Manybar **Goatfish** have a dark stripe that runs through their eyes and three dark stripes on their bodies. Their fins are sometimes very colorful. They can **CHANGE COLOR** easily. It looks like they have whiskers, but really, these are barbels which they use to feel around in the sand for things to eat. They like to swim near the bottom of the ocean, stirring up the sand as they look for food. Their Hawaiian name means "pale red."

SNAcK TIME! It was said that Moano turned red from eating red 'ōhi'a lehua flowers.

19

HAMMERHEAD SHARK
MANŌ KIHIKIHI

Keoki Stender

Hammerhead Sharks are gray with flat heads that look like the shape of a hammer. They can grow up to twelve feet long. Usually, they eat squid, fish, other sharks, and rays. They sweep their heads along the ocean floor and use their senses to find buried food. In ancient Hawai`i, Hammerhead Sharks were caught, their meat salted, dried, and **COOKED**. The Scalloped Hammerhead Shark has been seen in Hilo Bay on the Big Island, and Kāne`ohe Bay and Waimea Bay on O`ahu.

COoL!

Hammerhead Sharks swing their heads from side to side as they swim along the bottom of the ocean. By doing this, they can find buried food by using their electrical-field sensory system.

HAWAIIAN FLAGTAIL
ĀHOLEHOLE

John P. Hoover

Hawaiian Flagtails are silver. When they are babies, they have striped tails. They swim in dense schools during the day, above the reef. At night, they eat plankton. Younger fish can be found in tidepools. Their Hawaiian name means "to strip away" (hole). A person would eat them by holding their dorsal fin in their teeth and "stripping" away the body. These fish were sometimes used in ceremonies for "stripping away" **EVIL SPIRITS**.

HMmM! In early Hawai'i, Caucasians, because of their white
• • • • • • • • skins, were sometimes called āhole.

21

HAWAIIAN HOGFISH A'AWA

John P Hoover

Young **Hawaiian Hogfish** are black with bright yellow on top of their heads. Their dorsal fins look like the prickly back of a hog. They like to eat **SEA URCHINS**, crabs, and mollusks. Found only in Hawai'i, this endemic (native to Hawai'i) species is different than other species found in the Pacific.

Did YOU KNoW? The Hawaiian Hogfish is considered an 'aumakua (family or personal god) by some Hawaiians.

HAWAIIAN LADYFISH AWA 'AUA

John P. Hoover

Hawaiian Ladyfish are thin and silver with forked tails. They usually swim in shallow areas with sandy bottoms. Sometimes, people confuse them with **MULLETS**—other types of fish they swim with. But, they each have only one dorsal fin (the fin on their back) where mullets have two. You can see them at Hanauma Bay on O'ahu.

WoW!
• • • • • •

Ladyfish are not ladylike. They are hard-fighting game fish and will give any fisherman a good fight!

23

HAWAIIAN LIONFISH NOHU PINAO

John P. Hoover

Hawaiian Lionfish are striped red and white. They have long dorsal spines and their fins have **LONG SPINES** as well, giving them a "lion's mane" look. During the day, they stay hidden in caves and under ledges, but at night they come out to hunt for small crabs or shrimp. Their spines are **VENOMOUS** and are stretched out when hunting prey. Do not touch them. Their spines can badly sting you. They are most often seen along the Kona Coast of the Big Island.

NAmE CALLiNG

Lionfish are also commonly known as turkeyfish, fireworksfish, firefish, zebrafish and butterflycod in other parts of the world.

John P. Hoover

LEATHERBACK
LAI

Leatherbacks are silvery with two rows of spots. They are long and thin with a dorsal fin that has a black tip. Their skin is very **TOUGH**. They like to be alone but sometimes travel in small groups around reefs. Their spines are venomous and can sting anyone who touches them. Because their skin is thick, in ancient Hawai`i they were used to make small **DRUMS**.

CRAFTY
The skin from Leatherback fish used to be used to make fishing lures.

MILKFISH
AWA

John P. Hoover

Milkfish are long and silver with large dorsal fins and deeply-forked tails. They have milky-white **BELLIES**, which is why they are named Milkfish. Because their pointed dorsal fins look the same as a shark's, people sometimes mistake them for **SMALL SHARKS**. But very unlike sharks, they don't have any teeth. They are a very important fish in Southeast Asia because they are a good source of protein.

COoL! Ancient Hawaiians used to raise awa in fishponds—they were as important as the 'ama'ama (Stripped Mullet).

26

John P. Hoover

Moorish Idols are beautiful coral reef fish with light gold bodies, wide black stripes, and yellow accents. They have **GRACEFUL** shapes with long trailing fins that curve past their bodies and long snouts similar to the Butterflyfish. They often swim in **PAIRS** or small schools, and are fun to watch because of their shape and coloring.

NAmE CALLiNG

The Hawaiian name kihikihi means "curves, corners, zigzag." This name also refers to Hammerhead Sharks.

PORCUPINEFISH
KŌKALA

John P. Hoover

Porcupinefish have large heads and eyes making their bodies look tiny. They have black dots and spines that lay flat all along their bodies. When they are scared, they **BLOW UP** into prickly balloons. This makes other fish not want to attack or eat them. Not only would it be difficult to swallow them with all their prickly spines, but they are also **POISONOUS** to eat—especially to humans. If they are removed from the sea, they puff themselves up. During the day they rest under reef ledges. They are most active at night.

WoW!

Porcupinefish and Pufferfish carry a poison in their bodies that's deadly to humans. The poison can cause a person to suffer "living death," where the victim is conscious, but can't move or breathe!

PUFFERFISH
ʻOʻOPU HUE

Pufferfish have bristly skin and, just like Porcupinefish, puff themselves up when they are scared. They have **SHORT BODIES** with no scales. Stripebelly Puffers, sometimes called the "Stars and Stripes Puffers," have white spots on their backs and sides and stripes on their bellies. They are the **LARGEST** Hawaiian puffers. Their name in Hawaiian means "stomach like a gourd." Small ones can sometimes be seen in the ponds at Ala Moana Beach Park on Oʻahu.

WEIrD! Some puffers have skin that feels like Velcro—especially when they are all puffed up!

29

RAINBOW RUNNER
KAMANU

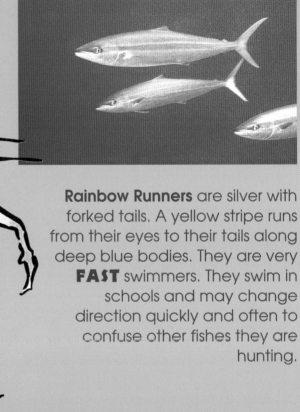

John P. Hoover

Rainbow Runners are silver with forked tails. A yellow stripe runs from their eyes to their tails along deep blue bodies. They are very **FAST** swimmers. They swim in schools and may change direction quickly and often to confuse other fishes they are hunting.

COoL!

Rainbow Runners rely on their speedy swimming to chase and catch other fish. They also hover near other feeding fish, ready to zip and snatch food away.

Keoki Stender

Red Snappers are pinkish-red with white bellies, forked tails, and upturned mouths, like a frown. They are a **FAVORITE** food in Hawai'i. Adults can live more than twenty years and some can get up to twenty pounds. Red Snappers live in very deep water and would most likely never be seen by divers or snorkelers. Forktail Snappers, Gray Snappers, Blacktail Snappers, and Bluestripe Snappers are the types of snappers divers would most likely see.

Did YOU KNoW? Their Hawaiian name 'ula'ula means "to make red" or "redden."

31

REEF TRIGGERFISH
HUMUHUMUNUKUNUKUĀPUAʻA

Reef Triggerfish—known in Hawaiʻi as Humuhumunukunukuāpuaʻa (the unofficial state fish) have colored lines "painted" along their sides. When threatened, they may swim into a hole to hide. Once there, two spines on their backs rise up. The first spine locks them inside their hiding place. If the second, smaller spine is pushed down, like a trigger, the first spine will unlock and the fish can be pulled out. Nukunukuāpuaʻa means "nose like a **PIG**." This is part of their name because when they are pulled from the water, they make a grunting sound like a pig.

COoL!

Because the Triggerfish's eyes are so far back on their bodies, they can easily eat sea urchins that have long spines and not get poked in the eyes! Now that's good eating!

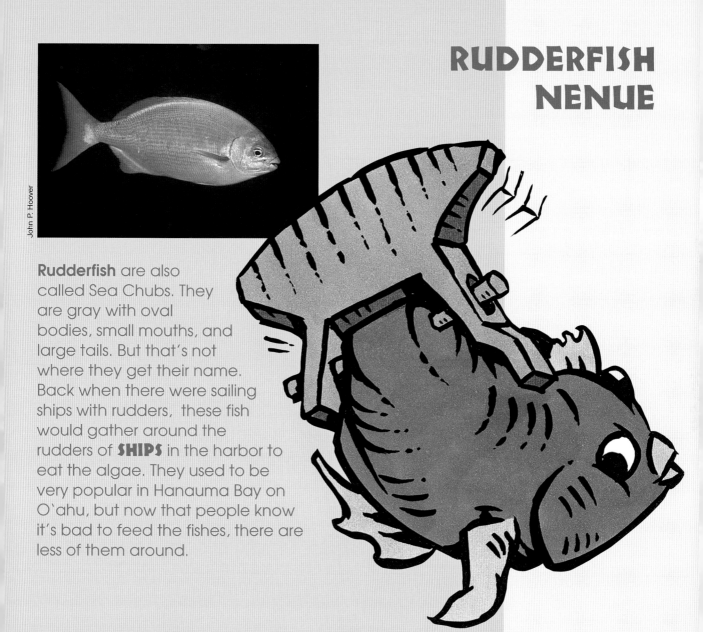

John P. Hoover

Rudderfish are also called Sea Chubs. They are gray with oval bodies, small mouths, and large tails. But that's not where they get their name. Back when there were sailing ships with rudders, these fish would gather around the rudders of **SHIPS** in the harbor to eat the algae. They used to be very popular in Hanauma Bay on O'ahu, but now that people know it's bad to feed the fishes, there are less of them around.

NAmE CALLiNG
Their Hawaiian name Nenue means "a paddle with a broad blade."

33

SAILFIN TANG
MĀNEONEO

John P. Hoover

Sailfin Tangs have brown, yellow, and white stripes along their bodies with large, **OVERSIZED FINS** that look like "sails." When scared, they stretch out their fins so they look bigger. Their tails are yellow. They swim in pairs and can be seen at Hanauma Bay on Oʻahu. Their Hawaiian name means "itchy." This might relate to the fact that when eaten raw, they give you a scratchy throat. They swim in pairs and, interestingly, the female fish are bigger than the male fish.

HMmM! Younger Sailfin Tangs have fins that are always stretched out—perhaps nature's way of keeping them somewhat safe from other fish.

SCORPIONFISH
NOHU

Scorpionfish have splotchy skin and venomous spines. If you are poked by one of their spines, it's best to put your wound in hot water to lessen the poison (or neutralize it). They are good at hiding themselves and blending into reefs or rocks. They are **SLOW** swimmers. So, they stay in one spot and when something swims by, they catch and eat it. One interesting fact about the Leaf Scorpionfish is that they shed their skins (like a snake or a bird molting its feathers), becoming a different color, sometimes.

YIkES! Scorpionfish are very good at hiding or camouflaging themselves against the reef, so if you do go diving, beware. Touching one could cause you serious pain or even death!

SKIPJACK AKU

Keoki Stender

Skipjack fish are silver with large yellow eyes and four horizontal stripes that run along their sides. They are fast swimmers and can swim up to 25 miles per hour. Sometimes schools of them can be seen **SKIPPING** and jumping when feeding. They are a favorite fish to eat in Hawai`i.

HaHAHA! Kids used to use the word aku to make fun of someone. AKU NOSE meant BIG NOSE.

Snowflake Morays have white snouts and light brown bodies with dark spots and **SPLOTCHES** with yellow centers. Most morays open and close their mouths to show off their needle-sharp teeth while sticking their heads out of their hiding places, but the Snowflake Moray does not have sharp teeth. Even though their Hawaiian name refers to them as fierce, they are actually tame and more **GENTLE** than other eels. (But don't let that fool you. They can still be dangerous.)

 King Kamehameha I was nicknamed Puhi Kāpā—but the name referred to an aggressive fighting eel, which does not describe the Snowflake Eel. It's possible that whoever recorded the name got it wrong.

37

SOLDIERFISH
'Ū'Ū

John P. Hoover

Soldierfish are usually red, medium-sized, with big scales and eyes. They go into caves during the day and "**STAND GUARD**" in front of their cave. But that's probably not where they get their name. It might be because they are red and reminded one of British soldiers (redcoats). At night, they eat crabs and shrimps near the bottom of the ocean. Big-Scale Soldierfish, pictured above, are the biggest of the Soldierfish in Hawai'i. They have white-tipped fins and large scales. They are sometimes commonly known by their Japanese name, **MENPACHI**, in Hawai'i.

INTerESTING!
· · · · · · · · · · · · · · ·
The Big-Scale Soldierfish was given a scientific name after Mr. E. Louis Berndt, inspector of the Honolulu Fish Market in the early 20th Century.

SPECTACLED PARROTFISH
UHU 'AHU 'ULA

Spectacled Parrotfish have a bar over their eyes like a pair of glasses. Their snouts are in the shape of a parrot's **BEAK**. Parrotfish swim fast and there are many different species with different colors and patterns. They are usually brightly-colored. They can use their "beaks" to bite off chunks of coral or stone—you can hear them scraping and crunching underwater. Then special bones in their throats help **GRIND** the coral into a fine sand making it easier to digest.

ZZZZZzZZ!
. . . .

Parrotfish sleep very deeply. In fact, you can probably pick one up and move it gently without waking it up! (Don't try this at home...leave it to the professionals!)

39

STOCKY HAWKFISH PO'OPA'A

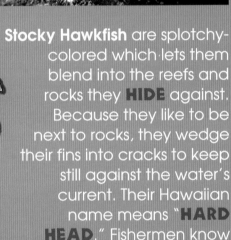

John P. Hoover

Stocky Hawkfish are splotchy-colored which lets them blend into the reefs and rocks they **HIDE** against. Because they like to be next to rocks, they wedge their fins into cracks to keep still against the water's current. Their Hawaiian name means "**HARD HEAD**." Fishermen know them as "Rockfish."

Ah HAH!
• • • • • • • • • •

"The fisherman who fools around in shallow water takes home a po'opa'a."—an old Hawaiian saying.

SURGEONFISH PUALU

John P. Hoover

Ringtail Surgeonfish may be dark or bluish-gray with blue fins. They usually have a **WHITE RING** at the base of their tails. Two sharp spines lie flat at this spot. When scared or when they need to defend themselves, the **SPINES** will flip out. Their bodies are oval-shaped and thin. They like to stay outside the reef and eat algae off rocks or sand.

WoW! Surgeonfish were named Surgeonfish because fishermen often got cut from their scalpel-sharp tail spines.

41

TRUMPETFISH
NŪNŪ

Trumpetfish have long, thin bodies. Some are gray or brown, while in Hawai'i, bright yellow ones can be spotted. They are the **MOST COMMON** predators on Hawai'i's reefs. Although they are easy to see from the side, head on they are almost invisible. They are sneaky when hunting. They swim with other schools of fish—like Surgeonfish or Parrotfish as a way to hide. Because these schools eat algae other fish aren't threatened. They don't see the Trumpetfish hiding until they attack! Trumpetfish can also swim next to other narrow objects, like a floating piece of rope, and hide that way. In the picture above, you can see two Trumpetfish. The smaller is "hiding" underneath the larger fish.

CHoW TIME!

A Trumpetfish's mouth can open really wide—wide enough to swallow a fish much bigger than itself.

UNICORNFISH
KALA

John P. Hoover

Unicornfish are large with a long horn sticking out between their eyes, and bright blue tails with "**STREAMERS**" coming off the tips on the males, only. When resting along the sand, they are a light gray color. But when they are swimming along the reef, eating algae, they are a darker color. Their Hawaiian name means "thorn." In ancient Hawai`i, their thick skin was used for making **DRUMS**.

INTerESTING!
• • • • • • • • • • • • •

The smaller of the Bluespine Unicornfish don't have a horn.

43

WHITESADDLE GOATFISH KŪMŪ

John P. Hoover

Whitesaddle Goatfish are grayish purple or red with a white spot above the base of their tails that looks like a saddle. They have white stripes by their eyes that run down their bodies. In ancient Hawai`i, these fish were **PRIZED**. They were sometimes used in offerings to the gods if a pig couldn't be found, and women were not allowed to eat them. The Hawaiian name means "master." When a student graduated and mastered his skills, a **KŪMŪ** was offered in celebration.

COoL!
• • • • • •

Many Goatfish can change their color quickly and dramatically. They might be one color while resting and another color when swimming. The white saddle doesn't change color.

Keoki Stender

Yellowfin Tunafish are large and silvery with bright yellow fins. They are popular fish among deep sea fishermen in Hawai'i and a **POPULAR** food. They swim in mixed schools of other tunas like Skipjacks and Bigeyes. The schools will often swim underneath larger objects like boats or driftwood. This might be because they like the shade, or because they are catching smaller fish that are feeding beneath the object, or it might be their way of hiding.

MMmM! 'Ahi is a VERY popular food here in Hawai'i. Lots of people like to eat 'ahi sashimi with some soy sauce and wasabi. Yummy!

45

ZEBRA BLENNY
PĀOʻO

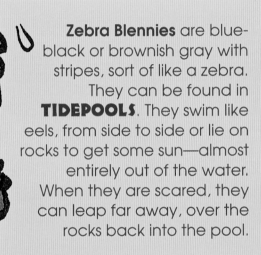

Zebra Blennies are blue-black or brownish gray with stripes, sort of like a zebra. They can be found in **TIDEPOOLS**. They swim like eels, from side to side or lie on rocks to get some sun—almost entirely out of the water. When they are scared, they can leap far away, over the rocks back into the pool.

FUn! Zebra Blennies do well in aquariums. Make sure you have a lid on your tank, though. They might skip right out!

SELECTED READING

A special mahalo to John P. Hoover for his insight and expertise. For additional, in-depth information, read these books and learn more about Hawai'i's amazing underwater world.

Hanauma Bay
A Marine Life Guide to Hawai'i's Most Popular Nature Preserve
by John P. Hoover
Mutual Publishing, 2001

Hawai'i's Fishes
A Guide for Snorkelers, Divers, and Aquarists
by John P. Hoover
Mutual Publishing, 1993

Native Use of Fish in Hawai'i
by Margaret Titcomb
University of Hawai'i Press, 1972

Sharks and Rays of Hawai'i
by Gerald L. Crow and Jennifer Crites
Mutual Publishing, 2002

ABOUT THE BOOK

This book was created because my grandson was always asking questions about the fishes we caught while casting or saw swimming by when snorkeling. All of the fishes had interesting names whether in their Hawaiian or English translations. Some were funny or intriguing and some even sad, like the Manini. So, the actual fishes themselves were my inspiration to draw them, trying to capture their true character without losing the likeness of the real fish. It was so much fun trying to think of ways to depict each fish! Plus, I think I learned so much more about them.

ABOUT THE AUTHOR

I was born in a small camp in Kawaihāpai next to the stone quarry in Mokulēʻia. All my childhood years were spent in the Waialua area, playing in the streams, picking wild fruit, swimming, and fishing in the ocean. Looking back, it was an idyllic and carefree life. As children, we never realized that life on a plantation camp was hard until we became teenagers. But all my youthful years are fondly remembered. A part of Waialua will always be included in my stories because it is part of who I am.

—Wilfred Toki

Wilfred Toki had a long career as an art director and, or vice-president for firms such as Tongg Publishing Co., Fujiki and Toki Design, Inc., Starr Seigle McCombs Advertising, and Reed Kaina Schaller and Strom Advertising. He continues to paint and is sculpting, by hand, stone poi pounders, bowls, and sinkers. His work can be seen in art galleries around Oʻahu. His two other children's books are *Hana and the Honu,* and *Moku and the Heʻe of Waimea.*

Bearded Cusk Eel

Bigeye Emperor

Bigeye

Bird Wr

Devilfish

Fantail Filefish

Flatfish

Flying Fish

Hammerhead Shark

Hawaiian Flagtail

Hawaiian Hogfish

Hawaiian L

Porcupinefish

Pufferfish

Rainbow Runner

Red Snapper